Writing the Wrongs

Poems About Recovery From Child Abuse

Al Johnson

Lulu.com

Other copies of this book may be
ordered from Internet website:
http://www.lulu.com/aljohnson

Al Johnson's website:
http://www.geocities.com/recovery_poetry

Al Johnson may be contacted via email address:
recovery_poetry@juno.com

Table of Contents

Introduction

From early childhood I was abused by my father, physically, emotionally, and verbally. The beatings were bad enough. I think, however, that the emotional and verbal abuse and public ridicule which I experienced left an even deeper scar upon me. I now realize that I will be on the road of recovery the rest of my life. I have often feared that others would damage me as I was damaged by my raging, critical father, but I have begun to trust people more. I tried to cope with the feelings of worthlessness that came from the abuse by burying myself in my work (my addiction, workaholism), depriving my wife and children of the time and love that they deserved from their husband and father. My job supervisor had to intervene and require that I get therapy needed to confront the ghosts of the past and my now unhealthy behavior patterns which once served me pretty well to cope with the terror of the abuse.

My counselor suggested I keep a journal to record my thoughts and feelings as I wrestled with the abusive past and moved forward in growth. Sometimes it helped me to journal my feelings as poetry. I thought it might help others to read some of this poetry.

This book is in two sections, this one, "Writing the Wrongs," telling about abuse which I experienced and how it impacted me. If you flip this book over, you can read the other section, "Righting the Wrongs," which tells about my journey of recovery.

Blow

The wind blows,
making big waves,
pounding
upon the shore.

Fist blows,
pounding,
make heart caves,
emptiness.

Wind blows
pass,
move on
and die.

Fist blows
crash.
Will they ever die?
Sigh!

Potatoes Sprout

One day little boy plays with his younger brother
discovering it's fun to sail 45 RPM records
through the air like a frisbee
many years before the frisbee name was known.

Oh, my!
One record amazingly sails
down the attic stairs
around the corner
into the living room
turns
and ends up against a window
sudden stop
cracked window!

Terrified little boy quits his play
and awaits arrival of his parents
who have gone shopping for food.
No more fun while sitting
waiting
in the living room.

Strong father arrives carrying
50 pound
sack of potatoes
to nourish
his family.

Eagle eyes
soon discover
cracked window.

Terrified little boy

takes responsibility
for sailing the record
that flew too far
so younger brother
won't get in trouble too.

Nourishing potatoes
are now used to discipline
little boy
repeated blows
with heavy sack
by strong father
upon body
of little boy.

Potatoes will sprout
and grow
more potatoes
if provided
proper environment.

Potato discipline sprouts
doubt
and terror
in little boy.

Cracked
window
was quickly repaired
by strong father.

Cracked
little boy
needed
repair
all his life.

Weird

W eird
E very day
I s
R otten
D irt

Sticks or Verbal Bricks

Sticks and stones
may break my bones,
but words will never hurt me.

NOT!

Sticks and stones
can break my bones
and leave long lasting bruises

And cruel words
are heard and mentally recorded.
The tape can play forever:

stupid
ugly
bastard
bitch
clumsy
weird
ignorant
witch

good-for-nothing
shorty
skinny
fatso
go-to-hell

We might more wisely choose our words
if we knew cruel ones wreck like rape.
It's lifelong work in either case
to repair our memory's tape.

In a Cabin

In a cabin dark and lonely
mother labored, thinking only
that our father shortly would come home.

She had cleaned and swept our dwelling,
though a dungeon, never telling
all the dreadful secrets hidden there.

Now she cooked her husband's meal,
waiting, trying not to feel
the foreboding that preceded his return.

As she toiled, under tension,
filled with fear and apprehension,
the potatoes she was boiling slightly burned.

She removed them from the fire,
made their water level higher,
hoping that her man would never know.

Soon she saw her husband walking,
nervous, greeted him by talking,
asking how his day of work had gone.

Sitting, hungry, not much telling,
he asked, "What is that I'm smelling?
Did you burn my supper once again?"

"The potatoes scorched while heating,"
she said. Then he started beating
on her head and pulling on her hair.

He'd raged before and now, repeated,
kicked her to the ground, defeated,
as she cowered on the floor and sobbed.

In a lull in her man's fury
she escaped, though could not hurry,
hindered by her pain of flesh and soul.

With blurring tears and glasses broken,
stumbling she hid. Groans unspoken
in the past swept upon her now with words:

"I'd leave my husband if I could,
but I shall not, because I should
stay on to help my youngster boys.

And if I took them all with me
he'd surely find us--it could be
worse than if we'd never tried to run."

So she returned to that dread house,
and shrank from woman into mouse.
We, her sons, have seen it for ourselves.

Caves

When I was a child
I was put in a cave
the door was held shut.
I panicked, in a daze.

I could not get free
though the doorkeeper was near.
I begged to get out,
but it fell on deaf ears.

The stifling darkness
stabbed me with fright.
I needed fresh air,
I was desperate for light.

My Hero also was put in a cave
just as he'd said,
his cave filled with darkness
of death—he *was* dead.

And there in my cave
it was deathly too.
I really didn't know
if I'd make it through.

My Hero came back alive,
He walked across his cave's floor.
His father was loving
and opened the door.

I pled for release
from where I'd been shoved.
My door, too, finally opened
but not out of love.

One cave was opened by a father
who loved his son, with pride,
mine by another,
with his own darkness inside

himself—locking me in the cave
still baffles me
but I'm learning to live
in the light since I'm freed.

Whenever I enter a cave
this is something I've found,
that caves ultimately open
although darkness surrounds.

My Hero and I both greeted the light,
the contrast with our caves was stark.
Outside there was freedom, freedom at last,
and welcome release from the dark!

I still fear dark caves,
I'm scared of tight doors.
But I know that my Hero
has been there before.

Thank you, my Hero,
for leading the way
from darkness to light
so I can live in the day
as well as the night.

Hide

Of the really Bad sins
we were not to commit:
    Don't smoke
    Don't drink
    Don't dance
    Don't go to movies
one was not usually mentioned
    Don't lie
but it was assumed that this
sin too should not be committed.

But
one day
for typical
Discipline
my hide
was tanned
beyond the usual
Hidden
places
where
no one else
could see the
physical
(not to mention non-physical)
damage.

Blood and scratches
appeared
on my face.

This was too much
for the constraints
against the Lie.

I was told
to say
I had fallen down the stairs
if anyone at school
asked me
what had happened.

I lied
not.
To save
the tanner's
hide?
No,
no one
asked.

And so
the lie
was hidden
but
my hide
was not.

And
we did not know
that we had
been living
the Lie
all our lives.

It wasn't
one of the
Bad
sins.

Temper In a Teapot

The water simmers,
gets hotter,
and finally boils,
temper in a teapot.

The temper boils over
scalding the hand
holding the teapot.

NGE

While others are blue
wishing they'd heard "I love you,"
my life's been rough
since whatever I did was
Not Good Enough.

Eyes

Old photos show adoring eyes
Toward your newborn child.

Blink

Old memories hold a picture of clouded eyes
Disturbed.

Disturbed turned to rage.
I cowered from those eyes.

Blink

After the storm,
the penance,
Shame in your eyes.

Blink

Eagle eyes watching every move.
I was intimidated.

Blink

The distant look, eyes far away.
Reliving? Remembering? Regretting?

Blink

When we say good bye,
Wanting to speak love,
An awkward touch, instead.

I see a tiny tear in the corner of
Your eye.
It speaks.

The Old House

Do you remember the old house,
with the windows stuttered shut,
doors armlocked so we could not get out?
Do you remember how dark it was inside?
Or am I the only one who can't forget?

Window Pain

When the death wish taps upon my window
I recall the tapping forty years ago
When small, I looked up to the starry sky
And wished, no, not that I could die,
but, rather, even more forlorn,
that I would never have been born.
It's hard to argue with the window pain,
But I'll resist: it taps more loss than gain.

Gray

Darkness descends,
surrounds, smothers.
Prisoner longs for light.
Day dawns,
but uninvited ugly
night and light
mixed in mind
produces persistent pain
of groggy gray.

Blackout

I've worn a mask so long,
  as well as protective armor.
They have kept me from letting you know
  who I really am
  and where I hurt.

Now that I've taken off the mask
  and wear more natural clothing,
  I long to tell you the truth,
    the naked truth,
  but when I speak I feel
    naked,
    exposed to your view.
I can't tolerate this,
  no matter how transparent I wish to be.
Your eyes feel like those
  prying eagle eyes
  of suspicion and condemnation
  that watched me all my life.
I can't avert your look,
  even if you mean it to be a look of love,
and so I avert,
like the ostrich with its head in the sand,
  if my eyes can't see you,
  maybe I am safe from yours.

I'm so filled with shame at my
  nakedness
  and vulnerability
  and weakness,
  as my world turns black
  and I faint,
  the blessed, shameful retreat.

Lord, your strength is supposed to be made
   perfect
   in my weakness.
But couldn't I trade this weakness for another?
How is your strength shown when I
   continue looking so weak,
   even having to take
   my panic pill?

Lord, please understand,
   and love me still,
   and could you, maybe,
   help some others understand, too,
   and love and accept me, also?
I'm stuck.

www.ingramcontent.com/pod-product-compliance
Ingram Content Group UK Ltd.
Pitfield, Milton Keynes, MK11 3LW, UK
UKHW041832200726
13854UKWH00003BA/1107

Righting the Wrongs

Poems About Recovery From Child Abuse

Al Johnson

Lulu.com

Other copies of this book may be
ordered from Internet website:
http://www.lulu.com/aljohnson

Al Johnson's website:
http://www.geocities.com/recovery_poetry

Al Johnson may be contacted via email address:
recovery_poetry@juno.com

Table of Contents

Introduction

I am an adult survivor of childhood physical, emotional, and verbal abuse. Thanks to the intervention of my job supervisor and longterm counseling, I began a journey of recovery. Over the years of this journey our marriage and family life improved and I am experiencing increasing joy and freedom from fear, fear which sometimes paralyzed me.

My counselor suggested I keep a journal of my thoughts and feelings on my journey of recovery. Sometimes it helped me to put my feelings into poetry. I thought it might help others to read my recovery poetry.

This book has two sections, this one, "Righting the Wrongs," which tells about my recovery journey. If you flip this book over, you can read the other section, "Writing the Wrongs," telling about abuse which I experienced and how it impacted me.

Someday I'll Cry

Right now it hurts too much to cry.
I can't deal with my pain.
Survival is my current goal,
Forget "No pain, no gain."

But someday when I'm stronger
And life is safer, too,
I'll look inside my hurting heart
As best as I can do.

And then the special child
That lives inside of me
Will face the pain, injustice,
And the tears can be set free.

I'll cry for the special boy
Whose childhood was lost
To the effort to survive,
I'll cry for what it cost.

I'll cry for others who like me
Craved love instead of strife.
Yes, in time, someday I'll cry,
For tears belong to life.

Unstuck

A snowstorm struck and we were stuck,
housebound for days. I missed my plane,
but relished hours for talking.
Finally a plow broke through
that heavy, wet, white glue
and I was free to leave.

My borrowed car slept, still
wrapped in its wintry quilt,
where I'd parked it atop the hill
in case the slope got slippery.

I worked hard to drive free,
but was still snowbound
when he drove up and scowled.
The air grew rank as in the past
when problems fouled a scene.

The trees had been whispering
but they hushed as disapproval
rushed from him to me. At last
I got unstuck and slowly drove
between those trees that always heard.

At the highway it was time to part
with our usual unspoken touch,
but to be silent now was too much:
I'd come too far for that.
Somehow, from deep within my gut,
three imprisoned words broke free
to accompany my pat
upon his aged shoulder.

He heard. He shook.
The trees leaned closer
to have a better look.
His face contorted
with generations of taboo,
and yet he groaned,
"I love you, too,
son."

I hungrily devoured those words
and savored them for miles as I drove.
It was worth traveling so far to get
unstuck.

Flow

He drew his sword again.
This time it pierced the skin,
and from my side flowed love
and anger, long within.

Resistance

Push against the darkness,
Lean against the night.
The demons cannot dance forever.

Shiver in the chill
before the sun's first glow.
Shiver, but wait for the day.

Boils

I covered the boil
with a mask, face enhanced,
and I felt the pain
when that sore was lanced.

One mask peeled off
where the lance had been aimed,
but another boil remained,
red, infected, inflamed.

I denied its existence,
hid it, too, with a mask,
but its day to tear off
came, a much bigger task.

The second boil was anger
which I'd managed so long,
but stifling that fire
just helped it get strong.

I'd known from depression
that I felt very sad;
I hadn't been aware
I was also boiling mad.

How do I feel, boils exposed?
Freer, yes, but also stranger:
It still seems odd
to view the pain and the anger.

Now I walk with these friends,
both well earned.
I'm farther along,
another lesson learned.

The boils are lanced,
but their scars remain.
Healing's on the increase,
infection's on the wane.

God's Tears

The storm clouds
  approach and
  engulf me
  darkening my world.
Then the raindrops fall
  from heaven.
God must be crying
  with me.

Safety's Smile

I'd had enough safety. I wanted free.
I broke water and struggled to the surface
gasping for the air of babyhood security.

A toddlerhood later that protection expired
and I was pulled to the water again.
Our boat kept us safe from the sea.

But it was a strange refuge,
drenched with derision and dread.
I tired of being so wet,
so, opting for water again
I escaped into the liquid chill.
There's three minutes to numbness and fifteen to death.
I died, and found safety, drifting numb for a boyhood.

A manhood later my own son arrived
and spotted me floating.
He boated beside me, smiled safety,
and said, "Come aboard, Dad!"
He reached for me and I took his hand,
emerged from the chill,
and smiled freedom and safety at last.

Epilogue

Many years have gone by since I wrote the previous poem, "Safety's Smile." I have continued to make progress in my recovery. But I have, at times, continued to be plagued by fear, a fear that sometimes has been paralyzing. The fear is triggered by the thought of eyes watching me, critical, ready to pounce on any mistake I make. Those eyes, of course, are the eyes of my father, which I wrote about in my poem "Eyes" which appears in the other section of this book. With my mind I have known that other people do not see through those same eyes, but eyes watching me have still triggered those lifetime feelings of fear.

Recently a counselor who believes that God can heal some deep wounds through focused prayer prayed with me, helping me address remaining pain. I had some skepticism. I wanted real healing, not some spiritual quick fixes. But I entered into the prayer time sincerely. We made important progress, praying about several areas that still needed further healing in me. Finally, we came to the issue of the eyes and how others might regard me as flawed, and I got stuck. I did not know what to do. My prayer partner told me to be honest in prayer. So I told God I was stuck and did not know what to do about my fear of the eyes, my fear of people seeing me with my scars and imperfections. And now, several weeks later, I still feel freedom over the gift that came next, which I describe now in the following poem, interestingly, a poem that connects to "Safety's Smile."

Piggyback

A grandfatherhood later
I got down on my knees
and smiled to my grandchildren,
"You can get on, if you please.
I'll give you a piggyback ride."

They rode.
They smiled.
They were beside
themselves with laughter
and I, with joy and pride.

A prayertime later
I was stuck in my past,
although I wanted to leave
the house of bad memories
that jailed me fast.

I was not able to move
through the door of that house
toward the freeing love
of the One I saw just outside
the door. He called me to come.
I told him I was stuck.
And then he came inside
and offered me
a piggyback ride.

The journey continues …